Bibliographic information published by the German National Library:

The German National Library lists this publication in the National Bibliography; detailed bibliographic data are available on the Internet at http://dnb.dnb.de .

Imprint:

Print and binding: Books on Demand GmbH, Norderstedt Germany
ISBN: 9783668455306

This book at GRIN:

http://www.grin.com/en/e-book/366665/impact-of-emotions-in-negotiations

Robert Neubauer

Impact of emotions in negotiations

GRIN Publishing

Emotions in negotiations

Seminararbeit

vorgelegt

am Lehrstuhl für Marketing

Technische Universität Kaiserslautern

Robert Neubauer

Kaiserslautern, den 29.05.2017

Content

Abstract

This seminar paper deals with emotions in negotiations. Both the negotiator and the opponent can use emotions in negotiations in order to influence the result to their own advantage. Emotions can be divided into positive, negative and neutral. Within these three types of emotions, there are different emotions that can occur, whereof not all of them has the same impact on the outcome of the negotiation.

Based on a systematic literature analysis, the emotions that can occur within these three types are presented and illustrated. This seminar gives an overview of the impact of the three types of emotions in negotiations and is specifically focused on the positive emotions compassion and happiness, as well as the negative emotions anger, anxiety and sadness. The aim of this work is to compare critically and objectively the different effects of the emotions in negotiations.

List of figures

1 Introduction

As discribed from Nürnberger (2015, p.8), negotiating is commonly described as a basic form, of getting something that you desire from someone. It is a reciprocal communication of at least two parties, with the aim of reaching an agreement, provided that the other side has both opposing as well as common interests (Nürnberger 2015, p.8). The main objective of the parties is to reach an agreement after having clarified the conflict of interests (Pfetsch, 2006, p.15).

Carnevale et al. (2012, p.53) suggest that there is growing evidence that emotional displays can impact people's decision-making in negotiations. According to Nürnberger (2015, p.16) emotions are part of a highly complex apparatus that helps us to assess facts and situations. They move us to do or leave something and enable us to react flexibly to new demands of the environment (Nürnberger, 2015, p.16).

Kopelman et al. (2006, p.81) and Nürnberger (2015, p.18) have identified three types of emotion, namely positive, negative and neutral emotions. According to Carnevale et al. (2012, p.64) positive emotions are joy, pride, admiration and gratitude, while Geiger et al. (2013, p.269) names joy, curiosity, compassion and astonishment. Negative emotions are according to Nürnberger (2015, p.26) anger, sadness and fear, whereas Geiger et al. (2013, p.269) characterise negative emotions with the expression of rage, anger, disappointment, sadness and fear. However, neutral emotions can be defined as showing no emotions (Nürnberger et al., 2015, p.18; Bosse et al., 2014, p.119).

These three types of emotions can be used strategically in negotiations to influence the opponents' emotions, cognitions, and behaviors (Kopelman et al., 2006, p.98).

Considering that emotions can be used strategically in negotiations, the question arises how these different types of emotions can influence the outcome of the negotiation?

The objective of this seminar paper is to give an overview of the topic „emotions in negotiations" and to work out the impacts of different emotions on the outcome of the negotiation. For this purpose the work is divided into four sections and subjected to a systematic literature analysis. The first section introduces the objective and aims of this paper. In the second section, the concept of negotiation is defined and the two different types of negotiations are characterized. Furthermore the concept of emotions is explained and divided into 3 categories: positive, negative and neutral. Here the positive emotions compassion and happiness, as well as the negative emotions anger, anxiety and sadness are described explicitly. These emotions were deliberately selected, since the results of the negotiation exit are very different. The inclusion of further emotions would go beyond the scope of this seminar paper. The third section focuses on the effects of the previously named emotions on the outcome of the negotiation. The effects of positive, negative and neutral emotions on the outcome of the negotiations are first presented in general, and the emotions that are to be presented are then addressed specifically. The seminar paper concludes with a summary and an outlook on the further development of the topic.

Methodological approach

A literature review was carried out for this seminar paper. As well as using Google Scholar, EBSCOHost, SpringerLink and EconBiz this paper also uses books and journals. The relevant period of this work is limited to publications between 1997 and 2016, since they contain the latest insights of this topic.

2 Negotiation and emotion

This section deals with the most important terms related to negotiations and emotions.

2.1 Negotiation

The Definition of negotiation and the negotiations strategies are the content of this section.

2.1.1 Definition of negotiation

‚A negotiation is an interaction between at least two parties trying to reach an mutual agreement on the compensation of opposing interests, within the framework of a joint decision making through the exchange of offers and information, from which they expect to achieve a higher benefit to their respective alternatives‘ (Geiger et al., 2015, p.226).

According to Geiger et al. (2015, p.27) and Pfetsch (2006, p.15), the origin of the word negotiation comes from the latin language. „Negotium" means a business, because a negotiator was originally a banker or wholesale trader (Pfetsch, 2006, p.15). Nowadays the original meaning of negotiation is not just focused on the activity of banker and wholesale trader. Duckek (2010, p.11) and Vetschera (2013, p.135) are the opinion that negotiations are omnipresent and can occur in everyday life like business, public as well as private lives.

2.1.2 Negotiation strategies

Negotiations can be classified according to specific characteristics like the type and number of involved parties, negotiation points, number of negotiation rounds and the direction of the negotiation (Duckek, 2010, p.11). For this paper especially the direction of the negotiation is interesting.

The direction of a negotiation can be described as a negotiation situation (Geiger et al., 2013, p.233). Burgoon et al. (2012, p.137), Nürnberger (2015, p.9) and Vetschera (2013, p.148) designate the direction of a negotiation as a negotiation strategy. For this paper we use the designation negotiation strategy.

In the opinion of Duckek (2010, p.11), Burgoon et al. (2012, p. 137) and Nürnberger (2015, p.9), the negotiation strategy can be distinguished in a distributive and an integrative strategy. Both strategies rarely occur in pure form, usually negotiating alternately pass through integrative and distributive phases (Duckek, 2010, p.17). In the following the 2 strategy types will be described:

Distributive negotiation strategy

Nürnberger (2015, p.9) describes the distributive negotiation strategy as a „Win-Lose"-strategy respectively „fixed-pie"-assumption, while Burgoon et al. (2012, p.137) denote this strategy as a „the winner-take-all outcomes". The aim of a distributive negotiation strategy is to claim value and maximize „the share of the negotiator in what is essentially perceived as a pie of fixed size" (Vetschera, 2013, p.148). According to Nürnberger (2015, p.9) the basis of a distributive strategy is a limited amount of objects which can be split to all negotiation participants. The negotiation area is limited in that the negotiation items are fixed and therefore the overall benefit can not be increased (Nürnberger, 2015, p.9). The distributive negotiation strategy can be very contentious, because the profit of one's party will always be the disadvantage of the profit of the other party (Duckek, 2010, p.17).

Integrative negotiation strategy

According to Nürnberger (2015, p.9-10) the integrative negotiation strategy is a „Win-Win"-strategy respectively a „two-winner-solution". Burgoon et al. (2012, p.137) describe this strategy as a „win-win-outcome". „Creating value" is according to Vetschera (2013, p.148) the aim of an integrative negotiation strategy. Commonly this strategy subject to trust and a reliable relationship between the negotiators (Nürnberger, 2015, p.9). Integrative negotiation strategies are characterized by the fact that the quantity of resources to be distributed is unclear in advance and develops only during the course of the negotiation (Duckek, 2010, p.17). In order for a negotiation to be integrative, Duckek (2010, p.17) notes, that a number of conditions must be fulfilled: There must always be more than one negotiating point, the negotiation agreement must be expandable and the negotiation parties' preference distributions must differ. In agreement with Duckek (2010, p.17) the shared profit can often be considerably increased by cleverly distributing and expanding the resources to be negotiated. If both parties are willing to act cooperatively, to focus on their commonalities and not their differences, to exchange information and ideas and thus to generate alternative solutions, they can exploit the integrative potential of the negotiation, that means to generate value and both benefit (Duckek, 2010, p.17-18).

The Harvard method is according to Nürnberger (2015, p.9) a comprehensive and widely recognized integrative negotiation strategy. The Harvard method contains four essential aspects which will be illustrated in figure 1:

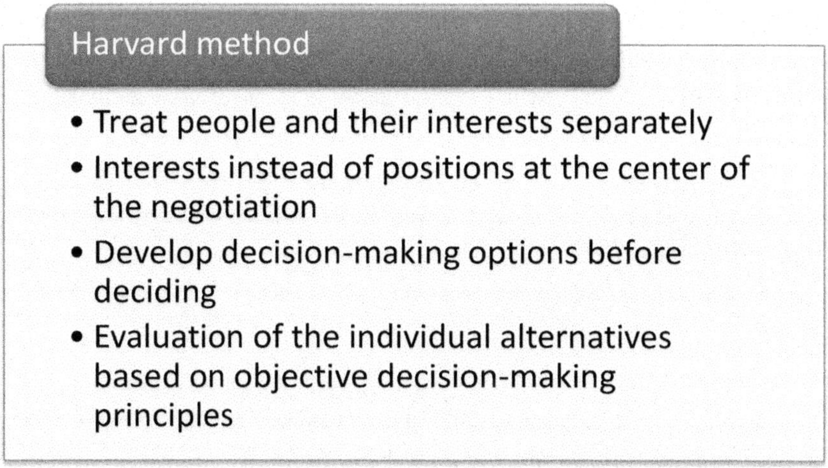

Figure 1: Harvard method: (adapted from Nürnberger, 2015, p 9)

These four key aspects of the Harvard method can be seen as recommendations for successful negotiating (Nürnberger, 2015, p.9).

2.2 Emotion

This section defines emotions and describes the different types of emotions.

2.2.1 Definition of emotion

According to Esser (2005, p.4) and Nürnberger (2015, p.16), there is no universal definition of the term emotion.

Esser (2005, p.4) is the opinion that emotions are states of inner excitation, which are connected with the fulfillment of biological and social basic needs, as an immediate and uncontrollable internal reaction to certain perceived stimuli in the inner condition or the external environment of an organism. According to Nürnberger (2015, p.16) emotions are part of a highly complex system that helps us to assess facts and situations. They move us to do or leave something and enable us to react flexibly to new demands of the environment (Nürnberger, 2015, p.16). Geiger et al. (2015, p.269) describe emotions as short-term, intuitiv reactions caused by a certain event or reference object, which can be relatively severe but does not last long.

The ‚word emotion dates back to 1759, when it was adapted from the french word émouvoir, which means „to stir up“‘ (Ploumaki, 2013, p.10). Jaakkola et al. (2014, p.540) characterize emotions as a short-lived phenomena in terms of their frequency, intensity, and duration. The main functions of emotions can be seen in figure 2:

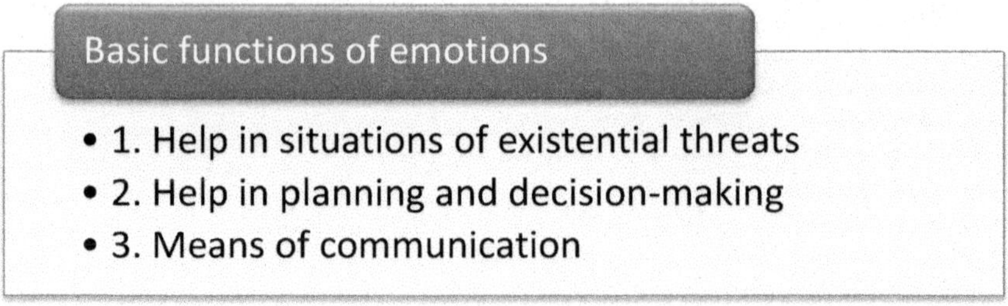

Figure 2: Basic functions of emotions: (adapted from Nürnberger, 2015, p.16)

Nürnberger (2015, p.16) explains the first point of the core functions of emotions as a help in situations of existential threats, because emotions trigger in fractions of seconds actions such as dodging, escape or freezing. The second point is according to Nürnberger (2015, p.16) a help in planning and decision-making because forward-looking thinking and acting are closely linked to emotions. A means of communication, which is the third point in figure 2, is the communication of facial expressions and posture (Nürnberger, 2015, p.16).

For this seminar paper point two and three are interesting.

2.2.2 Types of emotions

Within the emotions consideration, the opinions differ on the number and description of the types. Kopelman et al. (2006, p.81) and Nürnberger (2015, p.18) distinguish three kinds of emotions in negotiations: positive, negative and neutral emotions, whereby Nürnberger denotes the neutral emotions as pokerface emotions. According to Vetschera (2013, p.142) emotions in negotiations can be classified as „collaborative, aggressive or neutral", while Jaakkola et al. (2014, p.548) name 5 types of emotions: positive, neutral, dejection-related, agitation-related, other negative emotions. For this paper are three types of emotions from 0Kopelman et al. and Nürnberger relevant, which are illustrated in figure 3:

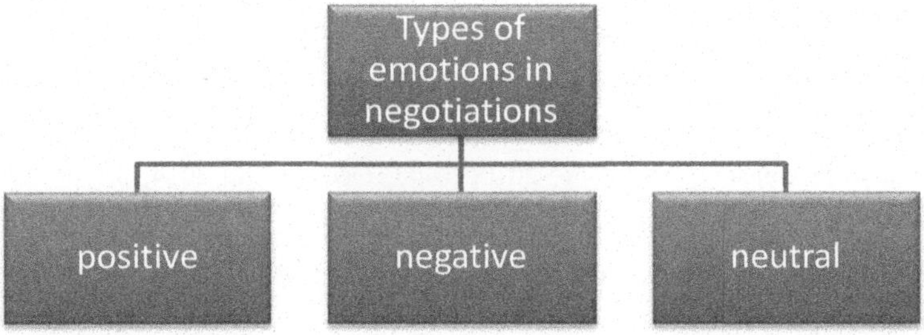

Figure 3: Types of emotions in negotiations: (adapted from Kopelman et al., 2006, p.81; Nürnberger, 2015, p.18)

In the following the three types are defined, explained and the relevant emotions for these types are assigned.

Positive emotions

Positive emotions are according to Kopelman et al. (2006, p.82) „vague and underspecified", i.e. ,they are more likely to occur when people feel safe and satiated and facilitate approach behavior, exploration, and activity engagement. In accordance with the opinion of Jaakkola et al. (2014, p.540) positive emotions arise, when it's possible for the negotiator to attain his goals and the procedure has been continuous. Filzmoser et al. (2016, p.1176) means, that positive emotions relate to flexibility. A friendly tone, often smiling, nodding the head in agreement and to be cordial and invinting are according to Kopelman et al. (2006, p.91) positive emotions that can be shown from the negotiator. According to Adair/Semnani-Azad (2014, p.69) positive emotions can be communicated through vocal warmth, vocal pleasantness, and relaxed laughter.

Jaakkola et al. (2014, p.548) name calm, driven, friendly, happy, quiet, relaxed and satisfied as positive emotions, whereas Carnevale et al. (2012, p.64) list joy, pride, admiration and gratitude. Positive emotions can also be joy, curiosity, compassion or astonishment (Geiger et al., 2013, p.269). Bosse et al. (2014, p.119) used joy, happy-for and admiration to describe positive emotions.

For this seminar paper compassion and happiness are relevant, which will be defined in the following.

Compassion

The involvement of empathy and „understanding regarding the other's intentions and motives for a past behaviour in that even though the primary appraisal is negative", is according to description of Liu/Wang (2010, p.445) compassion. Compassion can commonly used interchangeable with empathy (Liu/Wang, 2010, p.445; Oetzel et al. 2014, p.376). Liu/Wang (2010, p.445) extend the use of compassion with sympathy and pity. Compassionate feelings can result from the impression „that the other person is not responsible because of extenuating circumstances" (Liu/Wang, 2010, p.445).

Happiness

A state of pleasure, security and generosity, which is manifested in outgoingness and approach-related behaviors can be associated with happiness, whereas it can also been associated with a motive toward affiliation and social bonding (van Kleef, 2014, p.3). Carnevale (2007, p.60) and Govan et al. (2010, p.127) notes that happiness denotes satisfaction. Happiness can arise, according to van Kleef (2014, p.3), „when goals have been met or good process is being made toward attaining them and expectations are positive."

Negative emotions

In accordance with the opinion of Kopelman et al. (2006, p.82) „negative emotions represent specific action tendencies that narrow in on a specific subset of behavioral options and are necessary for survival in life-or-death situations.“ In consonance with Cheng et al. (2014, p.747) negative emotions can often be confrontational, while arising during the negotiation. A loud or sharp vocal tone, a fast speaking rate, and a negative affect in tone of voice can be seen as a medium for a negative affect (Adair/Semnami-Azad, 2014, p.69). A negotiator can express negative emotions while speaking antagonistically, appearing intimidating and being insistent (Kopelman et al., 2006, p.91).

Jaakkola et al. (2014, p.541) distinguish „two classes of negative emotions“: dejection-related and agitation-related. To be angry at other, disappointment, dissatisfaction, frustration, hopelessness, irritation, regret, and sadness can be assigned as dejection-related negative emotions, while to be angry on oneself, anxiety, apprehensiveness, ashamedness, fear, pressure, self-blame and tense can be authorzied as agitation-related negative emotions (Jaakkola et al., 2014, p.541). Additionally Jaakkola et al. (2014, p.548) name confusion, indecisiveness, resentfulness, threat, uneasiness and uncertainty as „other negative emotions“. Nürnberger (2015, p.26) and Bosse et al. (2014, p. 103) reference to anger and sadness, whereas Nürnberger add fear as negative emotions. Geiger et al. (2013, p.269) include rage, anger, disappointment, sadness and fear as negative emotions.

Anger, anxiety and sadness are relevant, which will be characterised below.

Anger

In accordance with the opinion of Liu/Wang (2010, p.445), anger can provoke „an intention in an individual to remove the barrier or decrease an unwanted response through punishment and retaliation.“ The communication of toughness is according to Kopelman et al. (2006, p.83, p.) and Filzmoser et al. (2016, p.1177) a display of anger. Filzmoser et al. (2016, p.1185) add resoluteness as an association with expressions of anger. The triggering of anger is often caused by other persons (Brooks/Schweitzer, 2011, p.43). In the opinion of van Kleef (2014, p.3) anger „arises when one’s goals are being frustrated and one blames someone else for it.“

Anxiety

Brooks/Schweitzer (2011, p.44) „define anxiety to include fear, frustration, stress, tension, worry, apprehension, and nervousness.“ If the term anxiety is used in the following, it includes sources with the term fear.

An ‚high uncertainty and a lack of control‘, as well as being „high in activation and unpleasantness“ are characteristics of anxiety (Brooks/Schweitzer (2011, p.44). Risk-aversion is pursuant to Kopelman et al. (2006, p.84) a typical behavior of anxiety. Jaakkola et al. (2014, p.540) associate this emotion with the „tendency to escape“.

Sadness

Signals that the expresser is ‚helpless and experiencing difficulty adjusting to the current situation is in agreement with the opinion of Haag et al. (2015, p.1848). Haag et al. (2015, p.1848) specify sadness as a call for help and a need for support. In accordance with the opinion of van Kleef (2014, p.3) sadness can also be an expression to solicit help. The trigger for sadness is typically a situation (Brooks/Schweitzer, 2011, p.43). According to Haag et al. (2015, p.1848) sadness arise ‚when individuals face a loss or adversity.

Neutral emotions

Neutral emotions are in accordance with the opinion of Kopelman et al. (2006, p.84) emotions, which are suppressed and concealed. This type of emotion does not elicit feelings or expressions from the negotiator (Kopelman et al, 2006, p.84). Nürnberger (2015, p.18) and Bosse et al. (2014, p.119) describes neutral emotions as ‚no emotion‘.

Synonyms for neutral emotions are according to Kopelman et al. (2006, p.84) and Nürnberger (2015, p.18) poker-face-emotions.

The three types of emotions in negotiations and their relevant emotions for this paper are highlighted in figure 4.

Figure 4: Types and the relevant emotions

3 Impact of emotions in negotiations

The third chapter provides an overview of the effects of positive, negative and neutral emotions in negotiations.

3.1 Positive emotions

There is a variety of research articles that have investigated the impact of positive emotions in negotiations. This resulted in many overlaps, but also some differences. All the impacts of positive emotions in negotiations, which were found at least two times in the literature found, are delineated in figure 5.

Figure 5: Impact of positive emotions on the negotiation

As shown in figure 5, Brooks/Schweitzer (2011, p.43-44), De Dreu et al. (2006, p.124), Filzmoser et al. (2016, p.1177), Geiger et al. (2013, p.269) and Van Kleef (2014, p.4) are the opinion that positive emotions in negotiation can develop a cooperative behavior. While Filzmoser (2016, p.1177) and Geiger et al. (2013, p.269) are speaking about an „increase of cooperation", the rest of prior named researchers are additionally speaking about a development of cooperative behavior. This increase for cooperation was noted, even if the positive emotion had been strategically deployed (Geiger et al. p.269). An improvement of information processes is according to Carnevale (2008, p.51) and Kopelman et al. (2006, p.83) an impact of an positive emotion negotiator. According to the opinion of Kopelman et al. (2006, p.83) are problem solving results the impact of the improvement of information processes and creative thinking. Another impact of positive emotions in negotiations is the increase in joint gains (De Dreu et al., 2006, p.125; Filzmoser et al. 2016, p.1176). Choi et al. (2014, p.478-479) call the increase in joint gains, as a promotion of win-win agreements. The increase of concession making is pursuant to Brooks/Schweitzer, (2011, p.44), Choi et al. (2014, p.478), De Dreu et al. (2006, p.124) and Filzmoser et al. (2016, p.1176) an impact of positive emotions in negotiations. The gain of concession making is closly related to the increase in joint gains, because joint utility results from concessions (Filzmoser et al. 2016, p.1180). The mostly named of the shown impacts of positive emotions in negotiations, is the stimulation of creative problem solving (Brooks/Schweitzer, 2011, p.44; Carnevale, 2008, p.51; Choi et al., 2014, p.478; De Dreu et al., 2006, p.124; Filzmoser et al., 2016, p.1177; Kopelman et al., 2006, p.83). Choi et al. (2014, p.479) add that the stimulation of creative problem solving result in integrative agreements.

Compassion

The influence of compassion is in accordance with the opinion of Liu/Wang (2010, p.449) interceded by trust, which stems from the perception that the object engaged in unsatisfactory behaviors due to the external occurence is beyond personal control. Liu/Wang (2010, p.455) and Oetzel et al. (2014, p.373) found that there is a significant association between compassion and the enhancement of the other's face. Oetzel et al. (2014, p.373) also mention that there was a positive relation between compassion and interdependent self-construal and the „integrating, compromising, and obliging styles". This encourages people to place more importance on cooperative goals (Liu/Wang, 2010, p.462). Compassion through trust has according to Liu/Wang (2010, p.462) an indirect effect on cooperative goals, including maximizing both parties‘ profit, promoting information exchange and promoting a positive relationship. Additionally, Oetzel et al. (2014, p.377) argue that compassion enhance joint gains while reducing distributive or aggressive behavior. A further impact of compassion in negotiations is the increase of helping behavior and the decrease of punishment and retaliation (Allred et al., 1997, p.177).

Happiness

Desired outcomes can be conceived as symmetrical effects when showing off expressions of happiness from the perspective of the person doing the expressing (Van Kleef, 2014, p.14). According to Govan et al. (2010, p.137) the expression of happiness reifies the power difference to the powerholder and signals submissiveness. There are different opinions about the concession when negotiating with a happy expression. While De Dreu et al. (2006, p.125), Govan et al. (2010, p.126), Carnevale et al. (2012, p.54) and Brooks/Schweitzer (2011, p.44) identified that negotiators who display happiness while negotiating make commonly small concessions, Carnevale (2007, p.53) takes the view that happiness can foster cooperation. According to Van Kleef (2014, p.10) there is a distinguishment between expressions which are directed to the opponents‘ offer and to the negotiator as person. While the expression of happiness, directed to the opponents offer, triggers a small concession, it causes a high concession, when it is directed to the negotiator as person (Van Kleef, 2014, p.10).

Additionally to the small concessions De Dreu et al. (2006, p.125) and Carnevale et al. (2012, p.63) mention that negotiators who have a happy opponent place higher demands. Commonly the negotiator infer the opponent to have low limits respectively aspirations (Carnevale et al. 2012, p.63; Carnevale 2007, p.53). An impact of happiness in negotiations can further foster concession making and problem solving (Carnevale 2007, p.53).

3.2 Negative emotions

The impact of negative emotions on negotiations has been examined by divers researchers. Like in chapter 3.1 there are certain overlaps and some divergences. Figure 6 shows all impacts of negative emotions in negotiations, which were found at least 2 time.

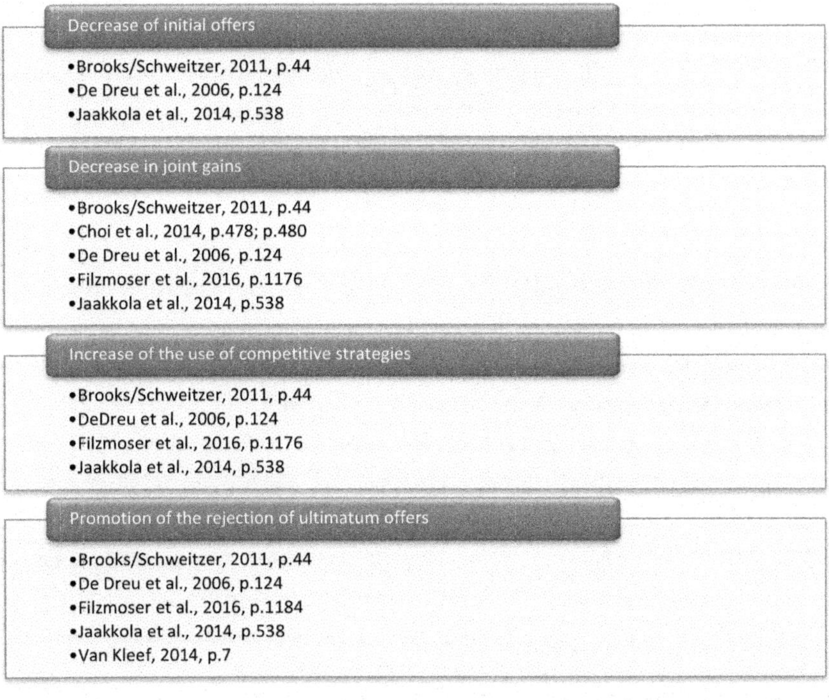

Figure 6: Impact of negative emotions on the negotiation

According to Brooks/Schweitzer (2011, p.44), De Dreu et al. (2006, p.124) and Jaakkola et al. (2014, p.538) one impact of negative emotions on negotiations is the decrease of initial offers. A further impact of negative emotions on negotiations is the decrease in joint gains (Brooks/Schweitzer, 2011, p.44; Choi et al., 2014, p.478; De Dreu et al., 2006, p.124; Filzmoser et al., 2016, p.1176; Jaakkola et al., 2014, p.538). While Brooks/Schweitzer (2011, p.44), De Dreu et al. (2006, p.124), Filzmoser et al. (2016, p.1176) and Jaakkola et al. (2014, p.538) bring up the term decrease in joint gains, Choi et al. (2014, p.480) is speaking about an reduction in joint gains, because negative emotions in negotiations can lead to inadequate outcomes. Furthermore Choi et al. (2014, p.479) allege that the prevention of a mutually benefical agreement is due to the increase of self-centered interests. Pursuant to the opinion of Brooks/Schweitzer (2011, p.44), De Dreu et al. (2006, p.124), Filzmoser et al. (2016, p.1176), Jaakkola et al. (2014, p.538) and Van Kleef (2014, p.7) is the increase of competitive strategies an impact of negative emotions in negotiations. It is to note that Brooks/Schweitzer (2011, p.44) and Van Kleef (2014, p.7) are talking about competitive behavior, whereas the rest of the priviously name it „competitive strategy". The last impact of positive emotions, which have been found at least 2 times is the „promotion of the rejection of ultimatum offers" (Brooks/Schweitzer, 2011, p.44; De Dreu et al., 2006, p.124; Filzmoser et al., 2016, p.1184; Jaakkola et al., 2014, p.538).

Anger

According to Liu/Wang (2010, p.443), the influence of anger was mediated by distrust. The emergence of anger can provoke an ‚intention in an individual to remove the barrier or decrease an unwanted response (Liu/Wang, 2010, p.445; Govan et al., 2010, p.127). This removal happens in agreement with the opinion of Choi et al. (2014, p.445) and Liu/Wang (2010, p.445) through retaliation. Punishment is according to Liu/Wang (2010, p.445) another possibility to remove this barrier between the opponents. There is agreement that the occurence of anger in a negotiation can decrease joint gains (Oetzel et al., 2014, p.377; Liu/Wang, 2010, p.465; Choi et al., 2014, p.479). By implication that means an increase of competitive behavior (Oetzel et al., 2014, p.377; Van Kleef, 2014, p.9) respectively competitive goals, such as wanting to get a better deal than the opponent, to attack the opponents face, and to gain power over the opponent (Liu/Wang, 2010, p.463).

Further, negotiators can be less accurate in judging the interests of their opponent (Liu/Wang, 2010, p.450; Carnevale, 2007, p.59; Choi et al., 2014, p.479). Carnevale (2007, p.59), Oetzel et al. (2014, p.386) and Haag et al. (2015, p.1859) agree that angry negotiator are self-centered on the one side, but on the other side Carnevale (2007, p.59) submit that angry negotiator can also go along with cooperation. This can happen, when the negotiator was forced to do concessions by an opponent, who was totally uncooperative (Carnevale 2007, p.59; Govan et al., 2010, p.136).

The display of strategic display of anger in a negotiation can claim value (Liu/Wang, 2010, p.465; Haag et al., 2015, p.1859; Kopelman et al., 2006, p.84; Govan et al., 2010, p.136; Filzmoser et al., 2016, p.1177). In accordance with the opinion of Kopelman et al. (2006, p.84) is the value claiming possible, only if the opponent perceives his alternatives to be weak. This peception is due to a tough communication of the negotiator (Kopelman et al., 2006, p.84; Govan et al., 2010, p.126/p.136). Due to the toughness in communication, there are also significant concessions to angry opponents, which has been introduced by Van Kleef (2014, p.9) and Govan et al. (2010, p.127). De Dreu et al. (2006, p.125) and Geiger et al. (2013, p.269) agree with the large concessions and De Dreu et al. (2006, p.125) bring up that angry opponents place lower demands.

Anxiety

Anxiety serves, according to De Dreu et al. (2006, p.126), as a supplication function, that means anxiety communicates dependency and a need for support. Additionally De Dreu et al. (2006, p.126) mention that anxiety in negotiations can elicit supportive responses and sympathetic in opponents.

Brooks/Schweitzer (2011, p.47) examined that, anxious negotiators can be seen as low expectations setter and low first offer maker. They also „responded more quickly to offer, and attained worse individual outcomes“ (Brooks/Schweitzer, 2011, p.47). Another impact of anxious negotiators is according to Brooks/Schweitzer (2011, p.48) the escape during negotiations.

However, Carlson/Dacey (2014, p.171) are the opinion that anxious negotiators are risk-averting and make despondent risk assessments, where pessimism is an increased probability of obtaining the downside outcome. Furthermore Carlson/Dacey (2014, p.184) show, that the use of anxiety can be distinguished between the loss in choosing threaten: small loss and large loss. On the one hand, instilling anxiety in order to induce risk-averting behavior is commonly ineffective, if the loss is small for an anxious negotiator (Carlson/Dacey, 2014, p.184). On the other hand, instilling anxiety in order to induce risk-averting behavior is according to Carlson/Dacey (2014, p.184) commonly effective, if the loss is high for an anxious negotiator.

Sadness

According to Haag et al. (2015, p.1848) and Van Kleef (2014, p.3) sadness elicit a concern for the expresser, which causes helping behavior. Moreover, Haag et al. (2015, p.1849) suggest, that the expression of sadness can also evoke reactions of compassion and empathy. Due to this helping behavior, negotiator commonly make large concessions to relieve the opponents pain (Carnevale et al., 2012, p.54; Haag, 2015, p.1854). Pursuant to the opinion of Haag et al. (2015, p.1854) and Bosse et al. (2014, p.102), an increase in concessions can only emerge, when the recipients perceived the negotiator as a low-power negotiator or anticipate a future interaction. Conversely, that means that expresser of sadness can claim more value (Haag et al., 2015, ‚p.1855). Besides this, Haag et al. (2015, p.1862) mention that large concessions can also appear, when recipients infer the relationship as collaborative.

Haag et al. (2015, p.1854) maintain that the expression of sadness can elicit perceptions of low-coping and opponents‘ other-concern‘. The expression of sadness can be effective when a feature of the social situation provides recipients with a reason to act on their other concerns (Haag et al., 2015, p.1854, p.1859).

3.3 Neutral emotions

It is important to mention „that the neutral emotional display strategy is not based in scientific theory or research, but is more of a lay-theory or prescriptive model of negotions“ (Kopelman et al., 2006, p.84).

According to Kopelman et al. (2006, p.84), participants with neutral emotions usually do more rational and ultimately more profitable decisions. According to Brooks/Schweitzer (2011, p.48/50/51) negotiators make, compared with anxious negotiators, higher first offers, stay longer in negotiation and answer more slowly to their opponents.

Haag et al. (2015, p.1854, 1858) suggest that opponents‘, who perceived the neutral negotiator as low-power negotiator, anticipate a future interaction and interpret the relationship as collaborative, claimed less value than a sad negotiator. Moreover negotiators concede more to sad opponents, than those who display neutral emotions, when the perception is the same as in the previous sentence (Haag et al., 2015, p.1862).

4 Summary and outlook

Summary

The purpose of this seminar paper was to provide an overview of emotions in negotiations, especially with the effects of the three different types of emotions. To this end, after the definition of negotiation and emotions, the most important emotions related to negotiations were described. In particular: compassion and happiness as positive emotions and anger, anxiety and sadness as negative emotions. It was important to present the effects of positive, negative and neutral emotions in negotiations and to summarize them with illustrations in order to give the reader an overview. Furthermore, the effects of compassion, happiness, anger, anxiety and sadness were consolidated and explained.

As a result of the impressions, it can be seen that both positive as well as negative emotions can have advantages in negotations. These depend on whether they are viewed from the viewpoint of the negotiator or his opponent.

There is agreement that the impacts of positive emotions: development of cooperative behavior, improvement of information processes, increase in joint gains and stimulation of creative problem solving has advantages for both sides. Whereas the increase of concession making does not necessarily have an advantage for both sides, but rather can be seen as an advantage for either the negotiator or his counterpart, because one of them must deviate from its actual negotiating objectives.

The decrease of joint gains and the increase of the use of competitive strategies as an impact of negative emotions in negotiations has a disadvantage for both sides, whereas the decrease of initial offers and the promotion of the rejection of ultimatum offers has just an advantage for the counterpart of the negotiator. It is interesting to note that the emotion sadness, attributed by many authors to the negative emotions has partly similar effects to positive emotions.

People are not machines and it is not certain that the strategy of a certain emotion leads to the desired result in a negotiation.

If a negotiator or his opponent is using an emotion as a strategy, it can nevertheless be that it does not lead to the desired result, since it is also important whether this emotion is against the person. A negotiation is always the interaction between people and it is never certain how the opposite reacts to certain emotions, because it is also dependent on personal attitudes of people or their daily form. Emotions may change during the negotiation and the other may not be conceived tot hat, so it is difficult to predict the outcome of a certain emotion.

Outlook

Emotions in negotiations is a subject that has been investigated for many years. However, it is noticeable that almost all authors limit themselves to the effect of happiness, anger or generally the effect of positive and negative effects. Positive emotions such as admiration and astonishment or negative emotions like disappointment and regret were almost never examined. Particularly in the area of neutral emotions, there is a need to catch up, as authors use neutral emotions again and again to compare them with another emotion and then distinguish them positively or negatively from the neutral emotions. It would be interesting to see a reasearch article, that only examine the effects of neutral emotions on the negotiation outcome. There is no overview of the different emotions and their effects on the negotiation outcome, so the research should deal intensively with further emotions and not only with happiness and anger.

Literature

Sammelband

Bosse, T./Broekens, J./Dias, J./van der Zwaan, J. (Eds.) (2014): Emotion Modeling – Towards Pragmatic Computational Models of Affective Processes, Heidelberg.

Geiger, I. (Eds.)/Kleinaltenkamp, M./Plinke, W. (2013): Auftrags- und Projektmanagement, Wiesbaden.

Pfetsch, F.R. (2006): Verhandeln in Konflikten – Grundlagen – Theorie – Praxis, Wiesbaden.

Journal

Adair, W.L./Semnani-Azad, Z. (2014): Watch Your Tone…Relational Paralinguistic Messages in Negotiation, in: International Studies of Management and Organization, DOI: 10.2753/IMO0020-8825430404.

Allred, K.G./Mallozzi, J.S./Matsui, F./Raia, C.P. (1997): The Influence of Anger and Compassion on Negotiation Performance, in: Organizational Behavior and Human Decision Processes, Vol. 70, pp. 175-187.

Brooks, A.W./Schweitzer, M.E. (2011): Can Nervous Nelly negotiate? How anxiety causes negotiators to make low first offers, exit early, and earn less profit, in: Organizational Behavior and Human Decision Processes, DOI: 10.1016/j.obhdp.2011.01.008.

Burgoon, J.K./Derrick, D.C./Jensen, M.L./Nunamaker, J.F./Twitchell, D.P. (2012): Negotiation Outcome Classification Using Language Features, in: Group Decision and Negotiation, DOI: 10.1007/s10726-012-9301-y.

Carlson, L.J./Dacey, R. (2014): The use of fear and anger to alter crisis initation, in: Conflict Management and Peace Science, DOI: 10.1177/0738894213501975.

Carnevale, P.J. (2008): Positive affect and decision frame in negotiation, in: Group Decision Negotiation, DOI: 10.1007/s10726-007-9090-x.

Carnevale, P./de Melo, C.M./Gratch, J. (2012): The Effect of Virtual Agents' Emotion Displays and Appraisals on People's Decision Making in Negotiation, in: Lecture Notes in Computer Science, Vol. 7502, pp.53-66.

Cheng, D./Doucet, L./Shao, B./Wang, L. (2014): Anger Suppression in Negotiations: The Roles of Attentional Focus and Anger Source, in: Journal of Business and Psychology, DOI: 10.1007/s10869-014-9392-3.

Choi, S.B./Cundiff, N.L./Kim, K. (2014): Emotional Intelligence and Negotiation Outcomes: Mediating Effects of Rapport, Negotiation Strategy, and Judgement Accuracy, in: Group Decision Negotiation, DOI: 10.1007/s10726-014-9399-1.

De Dreu, C.K.W./Mastead, A.S.R./Van Kleef, G.A.(2006): Supplication and Appeasement in Conflict and Negotiation: The Interpersonal Effects of Disappointment, Worry, Guilt, and Regret, in: Journal of Personality and Social Psychology, DOI: 10.1037/0022-3514.91.1.124.

Filzmoser, M./Hippmann, P./Vetschera, R. (2016): Analyzing the Multiple Dimensions of Negotiation Processes, in: Group Decision Negotiation, DOI: 10.1007/s10726-016-9477-7.

Govan, C.L./Neale, M.A./Overbeck, J.R. (2010): I feel, therefore you act: Intrapersonal and interpersonal effects of emotion on negotiation as a function of social power, in: Organizational Behavior and Human Decision Processes, DOI: 10.1016/j.obhdp.2010.02.004.

Jaakkola, M./Kumar, R./Luomala, H.T./Singh, J.D. (2014): When an Intercultural Business Negotiation Fails: Comparing the Emotions and Behavioural Tendencies of Individualistic and Collectivistic Negotiators, in: Group Decision Negotiation, DOI: 10.1007/s10726-014-9420-8.

Kopelman, S./Rosette, A.S./Thompson, L. (2006): The three faces of Eve: Strategic displays of positive, negative, and neutral emotions in negotiations, in: Organizational Behavior and Human Decision Processes, DOI: 10.1016/j.obhdp.2005.08.003.

Liu, M./Wang, C. (2010): Explaining the Influence of Anger and Compassion on Negotiators' Interaction Goals: An Assessment of Trust and Distrust as Two Distinct Mediators, in: Communication Research, DOI: 10.1177/009365021036281.

Oetzel, J.G./Ting-Toomey, S./Zhang, Q. (2014): Linking Emotion to the Conflict Face-Negotiation Theory: A U.S.-China Investigation of the Mediating Effects of Anger, Compassion, and Guilt in Interpersonal Conflict, in: Human Communication Research, Vol. 40, pp.373-395.

Van Kleef, G.A. (2014): Understanding the positive and negative effects of emotional expressions in organizations: EASI does it, in: Human Relations, DOI: 10.1177/0018726713510329.

Vetschera, R. (2013): Negotiation processes: an integrated perspective, in: EURO Journal on Decision Processes, DOI: 10.1007/s40070-013-0006-5.

Arbeitspapiere

Duckek, K. (2010): Ökonomische Relevanz von Kommunikationsqualität in elektronischen Verhandlungen, Dissertation Universität Hohenheim, http://link.springer.com/chapter/10.1007/978-3-8349-8678-8_4.

Esser, H. (2005): Rationalitätskonzepte, Entscheidungsverhalten und ökonomische Modellierung, Sonderforschungsbereich 504, Lehrstuhl für Soziologie und Wissenschaftslehre Universität Mannheim

Nürnberger, E. (2015): Emotionen im interkulturellen Dialog, Expose zur Master-Thesis Universität Kassel, https://www.uni-kassel.de/fb07/fileadmin/datas/fb07/5-Institute/IBWL/Wagner/Abschlussarbeiten/Expos%C3%A9/SS_2015/Expos%C3%A9_Elena_N%C3%BCrnberger_rev.pdf.

Ploumaki, M. (2013): The effect of Emotions on Business Negotiations, Master of Sciene Logistics University of Piraeus and Technical University of Athens, http://dione.lib.unipi.gr/xmlui/bitstream/handle/unipi/8410/Ploumaki_Maria.pdf?sequence=1

Lightning Source UK Ltd.
Milton Keynes UK
UKOW04f2018231117
313253UK00002B/370/P

9 783668 455306